Dedication Services for Every Occasion

_k, Jr.,_
mpiler

Judson Press ® Valley Forge

DEDICATION SERVICES FOR EVERY OCCASION

Copyright © 1984
Judson Press, Valley Forge, PA 19482-0851

Third Printing, 1988

The Scripture quotations in this publication are from the Revised Standard
Version of the Bible copyrighted 1946, 1952, © 1971, 1973 by the Division of
Christian Education of the National Council of the Churches of Christ in the
U.S.A., and used by permission.

Library of Congress Cataloging in Publication Data
Main entry under title:

Dedication services for every occasion.

    1. Dedication services.   I. Holck, Manfred, Jr.
BV199.D4D43 1984   265'.92   84-5695
ISBN 0-8170-1033-5

The name JUDSON PRESS is registered as a trademark in the U.S. Patent
Office.
Printed in the U.S.A.

Foreword: How to Use This Handbook

There are thirty-five services of dedication in this handbook. Each has been selected from the hundreds of such dedications that have appeared in the "Handbook of Dedications" of the annual planning issue of *The Clergy Journal*. These services, litanies, and dedicatory prayers should provide you with a basic library of resource materials for the most common types of dedications your congregation may want to celebrate.

Readers are encouraged to adapt these materials to local situations. You may duplicate, change, and otherwise use these services in any way you desire without further permission, providing duplication is limited to congregational use.

To use any of these services, you may want to select one or more that are appropriate to the occasion, make a photocopy, and then mark that copy with your changes. Thus, there may be litanies, prayers, and suggestions in several services that can be useful to you. Since the services are separated relating to the church building and church furnishings, you should find enough material in either category for almost any congregational dedication celebration. You may, of course, then arrange the materials to fit your own order of worship.

If a service you need is not listed here, please refer to the listing in the back of this book of many of the dedicatory services appearing in *The Clergy Journal* "Handbook of Dedications" over the past several years. A photocopy of any of these services will be sent upon request. Send your name and address with $2.00 to Church Management, Inc., P. O. Box 1625, Austin, TX 78767.

I invite you to send copies of your own dedication services to Church Management, Inc., for possible use in future issues of the annual planning issue of *The Clergy Journal* and/or in another volume of dedication services similar to this book.

Every effort has been made to give credit to the ministers and congregations from which each of these dedication services was received. We do acknowledge their contributions and thank them for their interest in sharing their materials with other clergy in this way.

Special events in the life of any congregation should be celebrated in special ways. I hope that these services—all tried and tested by various congregations throughout the nation—will be helpful to you in planning the celebrations of life in your congregation.

Manfred Holck, Jr.

Contents

Other Services

1

Ground Breaking and Site Dedication

MINISTER: "Who shall ascend the hill of the LORD? And who shall stand in his holy place?" (Psalm 24:3).

PEOPLE: "He who has clean hands and a pure heart, who does not lift up his soul to what is false, and does not swear deceitfully" (Psalm 24:4).

MINISTER: "Lift up your heads, O gates! and be lifted up, O ancient doors! that the King of Glory may come in" (Psalm 24:7).

PEOPLE: "And Jesus said, 'On this rock I will build my church, and the powers of death shall not prevail against it'" (Matthew 16:18).

MINISTER: And Jacob took the stone which he had under his head and poured oil upon it and called it Bethel, which means the house of God.

PEOPLE: And he said, "The LORD shall be my God, and this stone, which I have set up for a pillar, shall be God's house" (Genesis 28:21-22).

DEDICATORY PRAYER

DEDICATORY LITANY

MINISTER: In the name of God the Creator, God the Son, and God the Holy Spirit,

PEOPLE: We dedicate this ground.

MINISTER: For inspiration of our minds, salvation of our souls, and the illumination of our spirits,

PEOPLE: We dedicate this ground and give praise to God.

MINISTER: That here a sanctuary might serve as a spiritual beacon to guide our lives, inspire our community, and be a witness of our faith to our children,

PEOPLE: We dedicate this ground and glorify God.

GROUND BREAKING: (*Building committee members join with the pastor in using the spade. Others are then invited to take part. Young children may be invited to pick up stones and deposit them in a can provided for that purpose; thus they share in a "ground clearing" ritual. The congregation then sings one verse of "The Church's One Foundation."*)

THE LORD'S PRAYER (*In unison*)

BENEDICTION

As used in Christ Congregational Church, Miami, Florida. T. N. Tiemeyer, minister.

2

Service for Laying a Cornerstone

INVOCATION
HYMN: "The Church's One Foundation"
READINGS FROM THE BIBLE
LAYING OF THE CORNERSTONE

LITANY OF DEDICATION

MINISTER: To the glory of God our Maker, to the service of Jesus Christ and his church, and to the abiding presence of the Holy Spirit,

PEOPLE: We lay the cornerstone of this church.

MINISTER: For a building of which Jesus Christ is the chief cornerstone, the pillar and ground of the truth,

PEOPLE: We lay this cornerstone.

MINISTER: For a church that shall exalt not a religion of creed or of authority, but a religion of saving grace, of personal experience, and of spiritual power,

PEOPLE: We lay this cornerstone.

MINISTER: For a church that shall exalt the ministry of the open Bible, with its faithful record of human life, its unfolding of the redeeming grace of God through Jesus Christ, its message of inspiration, warning, comfort and hope,

PEOPLE: We lay this cornerstone.

MINISTER: For a church that shall teach and incarnate the doctrine that all are brothers and sisters as children of God, and that shall be a renewing and cleansing power in the community, and that loves every other communion that exalts Christ in the service of people,

PEOPLE: We lay this cornerstone.

MINISTER: For a church with an open door for all people, rich or poor, homeless or desolate, who need the help of God through us,

PEOPLE: We lay this cornerstone.

MINISTER: For a church that shall gather the children in its arms and hold them close to Christ, that they may grow up in the church and never be lost from its fold,

PEOPLE: We lay this cornerstone.

MINISTER: For a church which stands for the sacramental truth "It is more blessed to give than to receive," and which offers to people the abundant life which now is and which is yet to come,

PEOPLE: We lay this cornerstone.

ALL: In loving memory of those who have gone before us, whose hearts and hands have served in this church; with gratitude for all whose faith and consecrated gifts make this house possible; for all who may share this spiritual adventure in this our age; and with hope for all who shall worship in this house in years to come, we lay this cornerstone in the name of the almighty God, the Son, and the Holy Spirit, unto the ages of ages, world without end. Amen.

As used in First Congregational Church, DeKalb, Illinois. Stiles Lessly, minister.

3

Dedication of a New Church Building

(The congregation assembles outside the new building.)

MINISTER: The Lord be with you.

PEOPLE: And also with you.

MINISTER: Let us pray. To the glory of God, in thanks to the Lord of all for the love, concern, and untiring efforts of our general contractor, fellow worker and friend, blest and dedicated be this church building, in the name of the Creator, and of the Son, and of the Holy Spirit.

PEOPLE: Amen.

(Having come to the doors of the church, the minister shall speak.)

MINISTER: Let us pray. O Lord, God the Almighty, you are the same yesterday, today, and forever. Open our hearts to your discerning Spirit, that all our prayers and work may begin and end in you; through Jesus Christ, your Son, our Lord, who lives and reigns with you and the Holy Spirit, ever one God, world without end. Amen. "Lift up your heads, O gates! And be lifted up, O ancient doors!

PEOPLE: "That the King of Glory may come in" (Psalm 24:7).

MINISTER: "Who is this King of Glory?

PEOPLE: "The LORD, strong and mighty, the LORD, mighty in battle!" (Psalm 24:8).

MINISTER: "Lift up your heads, O gates! And be lifted up, O ancient doors;

PEOPLE: "That the King of Glory may come in!" (Psalm 24:9).

MINISTER: "Who is this King of Glory?

PEOPLE: "The Lord of Hosts, he is the King of Glory!" (Psalm 24:10).

MINISTER: Glory be to the Father, and to the Son, and to the Holy Spirit,

PEOPLE: As it was in the beginning, is now, and ever shall be, world without end. Amen.

SCRIPTURE: Genesis 28:16-19, 22

(Then shall the keys of the building be presented: The general contractor gives the keys to a representative of the Building Committee, who gives them to the vice-president of the congregation. The doors are opened.)

MINISTER: Since by the grace of God and under his good providence this house of worship has been provided to us that it may be set apart for its proper use to be a house of God, a dwelling place for God's honor, and a house of prayer for this people, we open it in the name of God the Creator, God the Son, and God the Holy Spirit. Amen.

PRESIDENT OF CONGREGATION: Peace be to this house and to all that enter therein. The Lord bless our coming in and our going out from this time forth and forever. Amen.

PEOPLE: I was glad when they said to me, let us go to the house of the Lord.

RINGING OF THE BELL

PROCESSIONAL HYMN: "Alleluia"

PRAYER OF CONSECRATION: Almighty God, whom the heavens cannot contain, but whose will it is to have a house on earth where your honor dwells, and where people may continually call upon you, be pleased to enter into this house, which we devoutly consecrate to the honor of your name. We set this house apart from all common and worldly uses as a temple and sanctuary of your presence, where we may gather for worship and fellowship; where we may celebrate new life in baptism and Holy Communion; where we may confess our sins and receive your forgiveness; where we may study your Holy Word; where we may administer the business of your church; where we may dedicate and rededicate our lives, our time, our talents, and our treasures to you;

where we may meet together as your family, to enjoy your gifts and blessings—food, drink, and mutual love; where we may come for quiet meditation and prayer; where we, too, may experience the presence of your Spirit, O God, and rise up to heaven in prayer, praise, and thanksgiving. Let the glory of God fill this house and the Spirit of God descend and dwell in our lives, through Jesus Christ our Savior and Lord. Amen.

DEDICATION LITANY

MINISTER: To the glory of God, the Creator, to the honor of Jesus Christ, our Savior, and to the praise of the Holy Spirit, our Comforter,
PEOPLE: We dedicate this house.
MINISTER: For worship in prayer and praise, for the preaching of the Word, and for the celebration of the holy sacraments,
PEOPLE: We dedicate this house.
MINISTER: For the comfort of those who mourn, for strength to those who are weak, and for those who are tempted,
PEOPLE: We dedicate this house.
MINISTER: For the sanctity of the family, for the purity and guidance of childhood and youth, for the renewal of fellowship, and the building of Christian character,
PEOPLE: We dedicate this house.
MINISTER: As a tribute of gratitude, of faith and hope and love, an offering of thanksgiving and praise from those who have found salvation and experienced the riches of God's grace,
PEOPLE: We, the people of this congregation, consecrating ourselves anew, dedicate this house as a temple, for the worship of almighty God, in the spirit and name of Jesus Christ, our Lord and Savior. Amen.
MINISTER: In testimony of our sincerity, let us unite in praying the Lord's Prayer.
THE LORD'S PRAYER
MINISTER: Thus we dedicate and consecrate this building, and rededicate its furnishings in the name of the Creator, and of the Son, and of the Holy Spirit.

HYMN: "The Church's One Foundation"
SCRIPTURE: Romans 8:11-19; John 11:47-53
DEDICATION MESSAGE
THE PRAYER
THE BENEDICTION

As used at Bethlehem Lutheran Church, Lund Community, Elgin, Texas. Alfred O. Hoerig, pastor.

4

Dedication of New Educational Wing

MEDITATION MOMENTS
PRELUDE
PROCESSIONAL HYMN: "Now Thank We All Our God"
INVOCATION
RESPONSIVE READING: Psalm 122
ALL: Glory be to the Father, and to the Son, and to the Holy
Spirit. As it was in the beginning, is now, and ever shall be,
world without end. Amen.
DEDICATION ANTHEM
OLD TESTAMENT READING: Deuteronomy 6:4-9
HYMN: "My Hope Is Built on Nothing Less"
NEW TESTAMENT READING: Colossians 1:9-20
HOLY GOSPEL: Matthew 16:13-18
HYMN: "Built on a Rock"
DEDICATION SERMON
CONFESSION OF FAITH
DEDICATION OFFERING
OFFERTORY RESPONSE
GREETINGS
PRAYERS AND THE LORD'S PRAYER
HYMN: "Lift High the Cross of Christ"

*(The congregation follows the processional cross out of the nave
through the new narthex and into the new multipurpose room
for the rite of dedication.)*

RITE OF DEDICATION

MINISTER: "Unless the LORD builds the house,

PEOPLE: "Those who build it labor in vain" (Psalm 127:1).

MINISTER: To your glory and honor, O triune God, Creator, Son, and Holy Spirit,

PEOPLE: We dedicate and rededicate this church building.

MINISTER: To the teaching of your Holy Word, to our growth in grace,

PEOPLE: We dedicate this church building.

MINISTER: As a place of fellowship, a place set apart for Christian nurture,

PEOPLE: We dedicate this church building.

MINISTER: As a place where people are loved, as a place where children and adults share the Good News of Jesus Christ,

PEOPLE: We dedicate this church building.

MINISTER: Where the citizens from the community may gather, where laughter and happiness may abound,

PEOPLE: We dedicate this church building.

MINISTER: As a place where young and old, the children of God, may increase in wisdom and favor with God and with all people, where service to others might be rendered in the name of the living Lord Jesus Christ, where generations to come might play, study, fellowship, and grow into mature citizenship on earth and in preparation for heaven,

PEOPLE: We dedicate and rededicate this church building and new addition.

MINISTER: With thanksgiving to God for the rich and ongoing history of our congregation, for the numerous saints of God who have given generously for this building program and for those saints of God who have sustained and continue to give for the mission of Christ Jesus through the ministry of this congregation,

PEOPLE: We give you thanks, O God, for your beloved saints.

MINISTER: We do now, as the people of God, set aside this newly built narthex, parlor, educational wing, kitchen, and multipurpose room and dedicate them to the glory and honor of almighty God and to the service of his holy church, in the name of the Creator, Son and Holy Spirit.

PEOPLE: Amen, Amen, Amen.

BENEDICTION

DOXOLOGY: Praise God from whom all blessings flow; Praise
him all creatures here below; Praise him above, you heavenly
host; Praise Father, Son, and Holy Ghost. Amen.

**As used at Gethsemane Lutheran Church, Austin, Texas. Karl A. Gron-
berg, pastor.**

5

Dedication of Stained Glass Windows

THE ACT OF ACCEPTANCE: Acting for the congregation, I accept the gift of these beautiful memorial windows with appreciation to all who contributed toward their purchase. We welcome the assurance that not only will these windows memorialize those whose names appear in our *Book of Remembrance* but also that they will enhance the worship of present and future generations of the people of this church with the beauty and grace of color and light, communicating the truths of God and the gospel through the symbols, leading us nearer to God in understanding and in service.

THE ACT OF DEDICATION

MINISTER: With gratitude to those who have contributed these windows and in appreciation for the lives which are memorialized each time we see them,

PEOPLE: We accept these windows.

MINISTER: To the glory of God who inspired God's children to bring the beauty of the rainbow into materials where it can be more frequently appreciated,

PEOPLE: We dedicate these gifts.

MINISTER: With devotion to our Lord Jesus Christ who has led us to know God and brought us the knowledge that in unity and in the light we may perform a higher service and more perfectly fulfill the will of God,

PEOPLE: We dedicate these windows.

MINISTER: For the artists and artisans whose hands fashioned and placed these windows, and whose skills and insights will eternally inspire those who worship here,

PEOPLE: We give you thanks, O God.

MINISTER: For those who through the centuries carried the message of the gospel through the world, in obedience to Christ's command,

PEOPLE: We praise your name, O God.

MINISTER: For the privilege which is ours, of being stewards of the gospel, workers who have no need to be ashamed handling aright the Word of Truth and passing it on to generations yet unborn,

PEOPLE: We praise your name, O God.

MINISTER: Almighty God, who has given, and who restores to us, those we delight to hold in memory, we recognize that you are the Creator of all things and in need of nothing, yet we desire to worship you in the sanctuary. Accept, we pray, the offering of these memorial windows and the lives which have been given to you in them; consecrate them by your power and blessing to holy use. May all who worship here now and in the years to come find inspiration in and through them and be lifted up toward you, the source of all being and beauty. This prayer we offer in the name of Jesus Christ our Lord. Amen.

As used in Prairie Avenue Christian Church, Decatur, Illinois. John L. Bray, minister.

6

Dedication of New Office and Study

MINISTER: In the name of the Creator, the Son, and the Holy Spirit. Amen.

SCRIPTURE: Acts 6:1-4

STATEMENT OF DEDICATION: Early in the church's history the disciples recognized the necessity of setting aside persons to do the work of administration. We set aside this day to dedicate these new rooms for the work of administration and ministry. Let us enter into the act of dedication.

LITANY OF DEDICATION

MINISTER: In order that the administrative functions of the church might be carried out decently and in order,

PEOPLE: We dedicate our new office and study to you, O God!

MINISTER: That the communications that go forth from our church might be an arm of outreach and blessing,

PEOPLE: We dedicate our new office and study to you, O God!

MINISTER: That the worship services which are prepared might lead people into deeper appreciation of you,

PEOPLE: We dedicate our new office and study to you, O, God!

MINISTER: That it might be a place of inspiration for the preparation of the proclamation of your word,

PEOPLE: We dedicate our new office and study to you, O God!

MINISTER: That it might be a place of healing for the hurting, a place of courage for the defeated, a place of peace in family crisis, a place of comfort for those in sorrow, a place of blessing for those starting life together,

PEOPLE: We dedicate this new office and study to you, O God!

MINISTER: That the memory of the work of those who are memorialized in furnishings might be perpetuated,

PEOPLE: We dedicate this new office and study to you, O God!

PRAYER OF DEDICATION: Dear God, who established the order of administration in the early church, we come to dedicate this new office and study, that the administration, secretarial work, counseling, and inspiration carried on inside these doors might have your blessing. We give thanks for each of the artisans who have dedicated their talents to create this place of beauty and efficiency. We give you thanks for those whose dedication of talent provided the finances to build and complete this project. Bless, O Lord, all the activities of our new office and study that they might be done to your glory. Amen.

As used by Wesley United Methodist Church, Pueblo, Colorado. Paul G. Tapey, minister.

7

Dedication of a New Church Kitchen

INTRODUCTION TO ACT OF DEDICATION: Inasmuch as our Lord Christ did sit and eat with men and women, boys and girls, in the fields, in the houses, and in the marketplaces of his time; and inasmuch as he invited all to come and share with him the breaking of bread and prayers at the table, it is entirely appropriate that we dedicate this kitchen, remembering the purpose for which it was brought into being and the greater good and the greater objective for the kingdom of God to which we here dedicate it.

SCRIPTURE: Luke 10:38-42

PURPOSE FOR NEW KITCHEN: Today, on this happy occasion of the dedication of our memorial kitchen, we would seek not to be troubled about the many things but to find that one thing that Jesus Christ has said is needful for us. We would here in this place choose the good portion which shall not be taken away from us, as Jesus has promised to Mary. This we believe to be the concept of Christian community and sharing, that each meal shared in the name of Christ becomes to us a sacrament.

STATEMENT OF COMMITMENT: Each time we gather and work together in this kitchen to prepare food, we are preparing acts of love and laboring together for the feeding of Christ's people, the church. If indeed, we as the church are the body of Christ, then we need food and drink, and we are grateful for people who prepare it for us. We seek to make for them adequate surroundings and a good place to work in their labor of love. In so dedicating this kitchen today, we not only honor those here present and those whose names we shall presently read in loving memory, but also we remember with affection and gratitude all the lives of those who have gone before us in the church—those who have labored in the other kitchen that was here before this one, those people who have gone now to join the church invisible and whose love and presence we have lost but for a while. They are a part of our fellowship at this dedication. We do, therefore, recommit ourselves to the service of feeding the people of God and, in fact, all humanity, through the biblical injunctions of Jesus of Nazareth, our Risen Lord.

ACT OF DEDICATION

MINISTER: In order that the functions of preparing food and sharing Christian fellowship may be maintained in a good and pleasant atmosphere, in balance and in order of both love and labor together,

PEOPLE: We dedicate our new memorial kitchen to the glory of God.

MINISTER: In order that people may find it easier, more efficient, better-lighted, and a more enjoyable place in which to work and prepare food,

PEOPLE: We dedicate our new memorial kitchen in recognition of a good design and well-executed construction. We thank our fellow workers.

MINISTER: In order that we may share in the solution to the problems of world hunger and the neglected people of God everywhere,

PEOPLE: We pledge ourselves not to be self-serving and fill our own bodies only, but to be more mindful of our Christian responsibilities to care for and feed the hungry of the world.

MINISTER: We hereby dedicate ourselves to a newer and enlarged vision of Jesus Christ and his body, the church, because we have this facility to use for the good of all people.

PEOPLE: We therefore dedicate this kitchen in the name of God our Maker, Jesus Christ our Redeemer and Brother, and the Holy Spirit which binds all together in one.

MINISTER: Hear then the names of those whose memorial gifts have made this new facility available and possible to us all. (*Names may be read.*)

PEOPLE: We receive this kitchen now dedicated to the glory of God, and pledge to use and preserve it by our prayers, our presence, our gifts, and our service in this church.

PASTORAL PRAYER

BENEDICTION

As used at Okemos Community Church, Okemos, Michigan. John E. Cermak, minister.

8

Dedication Service for a Memorial Library

MINISTER: "In the beginning was the Word, and the Word was with God, and the Word was God" (John 1:1).

PEOPLE: Glory be to you, O Lord.

MINISTER: "And Jesus increased in wisdom and in stature, and in favor with God and man" (Luke 2:52).

PEOPLE: Glory be to you, O Lord.

MINISTER: For the life and ministry of (*names may be read*) we are grateful.

PEOPLE: God's name has been praised.

MINISTER: The years (*names may be read*) labored among us were many, their spiritual messages were uplifting to us.

PEOPLE: God's name has been praised.

MINISTER: Because of their life and witness,

PEOPLE: We dedicate this library.

MINISTER: Because of the importance they gave to learning,

PEOPLE: We dedicate this library.

MINISTER: So that their memory might remain with us for many years to come,

PEOPLE: We dedicate this library.

MINISTER: O Lord, protect this place,

PEOPLE: And let your holy wisdom dwell therein.

MINISTER: The Lord be with you,

PEOPLE: And with your spirit.

MINISTER: Let us pray.

PASTORAL PRAYER OF DEDICATION: O Lord our God, the source of all knowledge and all truth, we thank you for the life of your servant(s) (*names may be read here*) and for the labors of love performed in this community. Bless with your heavenly grace this library, which we dedicate in the memory of loved ones named here before you, and to all who study here. May we, by the inspiration of your wisdom, love you with all our minds, and find in all created things the revelation of your glory, through Jesus Christ our Lord. Amen.

As used in Trinity United Methodist Church, Shelbyville, Indiana. Richard D. Clark, minister.

9

Dedication of the Church Sign

MINISTER: Just as Joshua established a marker where his people crossed over the Jordan, and as our Lord said, "Let your light shine before men," we, too, have built a sign to mark this place of the gathering of God's people; and, in a literal sense, it is lighted and does shine brightly.

PEOPLE: We proudly receive this sign to stand before the people of (*name of community or congregation may be stated*).

MINISTER: The sign which now stands before this building identifies us as a congregation of the (*name of denomination may be stated*).

PEOPLE: And we remember that when we depart and scatter to all parts of the community, we, too, identify who the (*name of denomination may be stated again*) are.

MINISTER: That which marks this place of study, worship, fellowship, and service stands in dignity. It stands before us modern in design, and complements these buildings.

PEOPLE: It shall remind us that we are of this modern age, and we endeavor to minister to its every need.

MINISTER: Although modern in design, it stands in simplicity.

PEOPLE: Our faith is for this age but not determined by it. Our faith also stands in simplicity. We believe that Jesus is the Christ, the Son of the living God, and we accept him as our Savior.

MINISTER: The design of our sign and marker is in the form of a shelter.

PEOPLE: Under the shelter of these connected roofs we shall

endeavor to provide a healing and nurturing shelter for the weak and injured. We shall be a people to protect and care for the world.

MINISTER: The sign before us is sturdy, built of wood and steel, anchored deep in the soil.

PEOPLE: We, too, make it our business to build our lives on a firm foundation and to be strong in the face of adversity.

MINISTER: Yet, that which we now dedicate is also perishable, and with time it shall be no more.

PEOPLE: We are also aware of our own fragile nature and we place our trust, not in that which we build with our hands, but in that which is eternal.

MINISTER: Let us pray. Our God, eternal in the universe, we thank you for this place of sacred meeting which gives cause for the erection of a sign to mark its place. And we thank you for the loving concern which has motivated the gifts making this memorial a reality. We thank you for the skill and artistry of design and construction which have made it beautiful and strong. We dedicate this, our church sign, to stand before the community as a symbol of who we are, the Christian church: dignified, contemporary, uncomplicated, sheltering, and strong, yet finite; we live in your grace and by your peace. To your glory we dedicate this sign. Amen.

As used at the Central Christian Church, Granite City, Illinois. V. Dennis Rutledge, pastor.

10

Litany for Burning the Church Mortgage

MINISTER: In (*year, the name of the church*) was founded by dedicated people to serve God and the people of this area.

PEOPLE: "Bless the LORD, O my soul, bless his holy name!" (Psalm 103:1).

MINISTER: There have been times of adversity, but they have been resisted. As Proverbs 24:10 says, "If you faint in the day of adversity, your strength is small."

PEOPLE: "Bless the LORD, O my soul, bless his holy name."

MINISTER: Preparation was made by people and pastor for a (*name of church*) future, remembering the words of Proverbs 24:27, "Prepare your work outside, get everything ready for you in the field; and after that build your house."

PEOPLE: "Surely there is a future, and your hope will not be cut off" (Proverbs 23:18).

MINISTER: In gratitude for the wisdom of our founders and for their gifts of land and money to encourage the work of God's kingdom in this community, we express our appreciation.

PEOPLE: We enter into this service of thanksgiving, O God.

MINISTER: Through the years the people of this church have echoed the thought of Nehemiah who said, " 'We are mortgaging our fields, our vineyards, and our houses to get grain because of the famine' " (Nehemiah 5:3).

PEOPLE: "Surely there is a future, and your hope will not be cut off."

MINISTER: The people at (*name of the church*) also felt as did

Nehemiah when he said, "And there were those who said, 'We have borrowed money for the king's tax upon our fields and our vineyards' " (Nehemiah 5:4).

PEOPLE: "Surely there is a future, and your hope will not be cut off."

MINISTER: We now rejoice together as our future of yesterday is brightened by the flames of a burning mortgage, and we know that our hope will not be cut off.

PEOPLE: "And all the assembly said 'Amen' and praised the LORD" (Nehemiah 5:13).

MINISTER: In our love for God and Jesus Christ and his church, and in reverent memory of those who have given us this heritage, we offer you our humble thanks.

PEOPLE: "And all the assembly said 'Amen' and praised the Lord."

MINISTER: In appreciation for the services of former ministers and members and friends of earlier congregations who have given fruitful labor, loyalty, and prayers for the advancement of the cause of Christ and his church, we offer you our humble thanks.

PEOPLE: "And all the assembly said 'Amen' and praised the Lord."

MINISTER: And now we, the members and friends of this congregation, offer you again our thanks for the privilege of working in (*name of the church*) and rededicate ourselves to Jesus Christ in the work of this church, in the extension of God's kingdom and in our community and world.

PEOPLE: "And all the assembly said 'Amen' and praised the Lord."

MINISTER: With thankful hearts we praise the name of God as we burn the church mortgage in the name of the Creator, Son, and Holy Spirit.

DOXOLOGY (*As the church mortgage is burning, the congregation sings.*)

As used at St. Andrew's United Methodist Church, Palo Alto, California. Lester L. Haws, minister.

11

Litany for the Anniversary of Building the Sanctuary

MINISTER: For those whose faith, courage, Christian conviction, diligent effort, and financial sacrifice resulted in the building of this house of worship,

PEOPLE: We thank you, O God.

MINISTER: For all those people of God who have led your people in worship here, who have preached your word from this pulpit, and who have administered the sacraments to waiting and believing hearts,

PEOPLE: We thank you, O God.

MINISTER: For all those who have come to this place seeking you and who, in worshiping you in spirit and in truth, have found you,

PEOPLE: We thank you, O God.

MINISTER: For those who have brought their children here for Christian baptism, for those who have pledged their love to one another at your holy altar, and for those who in Christian faith and trust have here parted with a loved one and committed that loved one to your love and care,

PEOPLE: We thank you, O God.

MINISTER: For all those who have here confessed their faith in Jesus Christ, have united with the church, and have committed themselves to the Christian life,

PEOPLE: We thank you, O God.

MINISTER: For sins that have been confessed and forgiven here, for burdens that have been made easier to carry, for distressed and troubled hearts that have known the peace

that passes all understanding, and for lives that have been inspired to new heights of love and of service,
PEOPLE: We thank you, O God.
ALL: For all your goodness and love revealed to us in this house of worship, we praise you and thank you, O God.

As used at the Community Church of Watertown, Massachusetts. Ernest O. Geigis, minister.

12

Rededication of a Church Building

(*Statement for Worship Bulletin*)

We rejoice in the completion of the project of renovation of our church sanctuary. As we come together today—old friends and present members—we give thanks for this expression of God's providence in a house for our worship, a home for our spiritual renewal.

PRELUDE

PROCESSIONAL HYMN: "Joyful, Joyful, We Adore Thee"

MINISTER: "Unless the LORD builds the house, those who build it labor in vain" (Psalm 127:1).

PEOPLE: "I was glad when they said to me, 'Let us go to the house of the LORD.' Our feet have been standing within your gates" (Psalm 122:1-2).

MINISTER: Let us give thanks to the name of the Lord, let us pray for peace, prosperity, and security as we worship together.

PRAYER (*in unison*): Almighty God, you who have designed and created the heavens and the earth, you who have placed your image upon us that we seek knowledge and wisdom, beauty and truth, we should ask that today you would grant us the presence of your Spirit, as we bring the offering of this renewed sanctuary unto you for your blessing. Help us that we may honor all those who have aided the building of this church in the past, by rededicating this building today, and giving it to those who will use it in the future. We rejoice in your presence. Amen.

ANTHEM
SCRIPTURE: 2 Chronicles 6:13-14, 18-21; Acts 17:22-31
HYMN: "Now Thank We All Our God"

DEDICATION IN PRAYER AND COMMITMENT

MINISTER: We rejoice together, members and friends of this congregation, and reconsecrate this chancel and church to the glory of God our Creator, Redeemer, and Sanctifier.

PEOPLE: Glory be to God the Almighty, and to the Son, and to the Holy Spirit.

MINISTER: For the worship of God in prayer and praise, for the ministry of the spoken word, and for the celebration of the sacraments,

PEOPLE: We rededicate not only this structure of wood and brick, but also the human building blocks of the church, its people.

MINISTER: For the remembrance of the seasons of the church and of human life, for times of preparation and birth, for times of penitence and renewal, for times of growth and life, for times of sorrow and death, for the time of life reborn, renewed, resurrected,

PEOPLE: We rededicate this house of worship where the rituals of life are celebrated and hallowed.

MINISTER: For the recognition of our unity in love, faith, and hope, in those richer moments of life when we reach out beyond our own,

PEOPLE: We rededicate the house of God in this place, that it may remind us ever that we shall worship God in spirit and truth.

DEDICATION HYMN: "The Church's One Foundation"
ANTHEM
SERMON: The Cost and Joy of Discipleship (Luke 14:25-35).
HYMN: "O Master Workman of the Race"
OFFERING AND OFFERTORY
DOXOLOGY
PRAYER OF DEDICATION

___

LORD'S PRAYER
BENEDICTION
RECESSIONAL HYMN: "God of Grace"
POSTLUDE

As used at St. Paul's United Church of Christ, Henderson, Minnesota.

13

Litany for Closing a Sanctuary

MINISTER: Let us give thanks to almighty God for mercies bestowed here in past years. For the erection and dedication of this house to your honor and glory as a place of worship, teaching, and service, and for the witness in faith and life which has here been given to the people of these generations,

PEOPLE: We thank you, Lord.

MINISTER: For all those servants of God who have led your people in worship here, who have preached your Word from this pulpit, and who have administered the sacraments to waiting and believing hearts,

PEOPLE: We thank you, Lord.

MINISTER: For sacred song and music, for drama and story and ceremony which have helped people see the objectives and directions of Christian living,

PEOPLE: We thank you, Lord.

MINISTER: For all those who have come to this place seeking you, and who, in worshiping you in spirit and in truth, have found you,

PEOPLE: We thank you, Lord.

MINISTER: For those who have brought their children here for Christian baptism, for those who have pledged their love to one another at your holy altar, and for those who in Christian faith and trust have here parted with a loved one and committed that loved one to your love and care,

PEOPLE: We thank you, Lord.

MINISTER: For sins that have been confessed and forgiven

here, for burdens that have been made easier to carry, for distressed and troubled hearts that have known the peace that passes all understanding, and for lives that have been inspired to new heights of love and of service,

PEOPLE: We thank you, Lord.

MINISTER: For all this building has meant to congregation, visitor, and town; for the walls of security, the overarching of love, the support of encouragement, the halls of friendship, the lessons of humanity, the lights of faith, and the doorways to service,

PEOPLE: We thank you, Lord.

MINISTER: Bless us, we pray, as we go from here; and, as our new church home grows about us, may we be bound together in the glorious adventure of building for you a house of life and heart and service, to the glory of your name and the extending of your kingdom, in the name of the Creator, and of the Son, and of the Holy Spirit.

ALL: Now unto him who is able to keep us from falling, and to present us faultless before the presence of his glory with exceeding joy, to the wise God our Savior, be glory and majesty, dominion and power, both now and forever.

MINISTER (*as all stand*): The grace of our Lord Jesus Christ, the love of God, and the communion of the Holy Spirit, be with you, evermore. Amen.

(*The minister hands the pulpit Bible to the president of the congregation and the official board escorts it from the sanctuary. The Bible represents the people's place of worship, and this action shows that the place of worship will be in the care of the official board until the dedication of a new building, at which time it will be placed on the pulpit of the new church home.*)

As used at St. Andrew's United Church, Truro, Nova Scotia. George H. MacLean, minister.

14

Dedication of Chancel Memorials

The Lectern

MINISTER: Dearly beloved, we learn from the holy Scriptures that it is meet and right that we should set apart that which we use for the worship of God and dedicate such to religious uses. We are, therefore, now assembled for the purpose of dedicating the lectern and the other gifts and memorials. The Lord is in his holy temple.

PEOPLE: "Let all the earth keep silence before him" (Habakkuk 2:20).

MINISTER: "I saw the Lord sitting upon a throne, high and lifted up; and his train filled the temple" (Isaiah 6:1). And one of the seraphim cried unto another, saying:

ALL: "Holy, holy, holy is the LORD of hosts; the whole earth is full of his glory" (Isaiah 6:3). Glory be to you, O Lord most high. Amen.

MINISTER: Jesus went about all the cities and villages, teaching in their synagogues, and preaching the gospel of the kingdom.

PEOPLE: "But how are people to call upon him in whom they have not believed? And how are they to believe in him of whom they have never heard?" (Romans 10:14).

MINISTER: The Scripture declares, " 'How beautiful are the feet of those who preach good news!' " (Romans 10:15). To the task of holding the word of God,

PEOPLE: We dedicate this lectern.

MINISTER: To the proclaiming of the Good News of the gospel

of Jesus Christ through the reading of the Scriptures,

PEOPLE: We dedicate this lectern.

MINISTER: To the inspiring, awakening, and comforting of the souls of people, that the people may be fed with spiritual food,

PEOPLE: We dedicate this lectern.

MINISTER: To the glory of God and the service of people and in grateful memory of those whose gifts have made this lectern possible,

PEOPLE: We dedicate this lectern.

The Book of Remembrance

MINISTER: For many generations monuments have been raised to honor the memory of valiant spirits. Among believers such memorials may well find a place in the house of God. This practice confirms the assurance that cherished human relationships are abiding when our lives are hid with Christ in God. Now and in years to come, when devoted members and friends establish memorials in this house of God, the names of these shall be inscribed in this book as an imperishable record. To the glory of God, author of all goodness and beauty, giver of all skill of mind and heart,

PEOPLE: We dedicate this *Book of Remembrance*.

MINISTER: In gratitude to God who calls us to bring unto him full devotion and before whom is forever spread the record of those who love the Lord,

PEOPLE: We dedicate this *Book of Remembrance*.

MINISTER: To bear testimony to the love of those who in the past and in the future shall set up memorials in this house of God,

PEOPLE: We dedicate this *Book of Remembrance*.

The Clergy Stall

MINISTER: The clergy stall which has been placed here for our use in the regular worship of God on every Lord's day,

PEOPLE: We dedicate to the glory of God.

The Dossal

MINISTER: That this aid to beauty-of-worship may lead all to desire "the beauty of the Lord," reminding all of the beauty of him who is "altogether lovely, the fairest among ten thousand,"

PEOPLE: We dedicate this dossal.

MINISTER: That the color before us may remind all of the deep red of the sacrificial living of those of all time who have followed the Christ of Calvary,

PEOPLE: We dedicate this dossal.

MINISTER: This dossal, the loving gift of (*here may be named the donor*) is given in gratitude to almighty God for the many opportunities to serve in this church.

PEOPLE: In gratitude we dedicate this dossal.

The Missal Bible

MINISTER: We rejoice that God in infinite wisdom has revealed divine truths to us in this holy book.

PEOPLE: "All scripture is inspired by God and profitable for teaching, for reproof, for correction, and for training in righteousness" (2 Timothy 3:16).

MINISTER: "How can a young man keep his way pure? By guarding it according to your word" (Psalm 119:9).

PEOPLE: "With my whole heart have I sought you, let me not wander from your commandments!" (v.10).

MINISTER: "I have laid up your word in my heart, that I might not sin against you" (v.11).

PEOPLE: "Blessed are you, O LORD, teach me your statutes!" (v.12).

MINISTER: "In the way of your testimonies I delight as much as in all riches" (v.14).

PEOPLE: "I will meditate on your precepts and fix my eyes on your ways" (v.15).

MINISTER: "I will delight in your statutes, I will not forget your word" (v.16).

PEOPLE: "The law of the LORD is perfect, reviving the soul; the testimony of the LORD is sure, making wise the simple" (Psalm 19:7).

MINISTER: To the glory of God, our wondrous Creator; to the praise of God, through Jesus Christ our Lord, and to the power of God, by the Holy Spirit, our comforter, both now and forever.

PEOPLE: We dedicate this Bible.

The Candlesticks

MINISTER: Our Lord said, "Neither [does one] light a candle and put it under a bushel, but on a candlestick; and it giveth light unto all that are in the house" (Matthew 5:15, KJV).

PEOPLE: We dedicate these candlesticks.

MINISTER: One we may look upon as a symbol of the Word of God, read and proclaimed in this sanctuary, which Word is a lamp unto our feet and a light unto our path.

PEOPLE: We dedicate this candlestick.

MINISTER: The other we may look upon as a symbol of the Son of God, who said, " 'I am the light of the world; he who follows me will not walk in darkness, but will have the light of life' " (John 8:12).

PEOPLE: We dedicate this candlestick.

MINISTER: We remember also the words of our Master, how he said, " 'You are the light of the world. . . . Let your light so shine before men that they may see your good works and give glory to your Father who is in heaven' " (Matthew 5:14, 16).

PEOPLE: We dedicate these candlesticks.

The Paraments

MINISTER: The rich colors and symbolism of the paraments are constant reminders of great truths and doctrines, and add beauty and dignity to the services of the church.

PEOPLE: We dedicate these paraments.

MINISTER: The violet parament, symbolizing penitence, is appropriately used during the seasons of Advent and Lent. Green, setting forth the teeming fecundity of all nature, is used throughout a long period to denote the Holy Trinity. Red, the color of blood or fire, is the color used at special times of remembrance. White, the color of purity and truth, is used at Christmas, Easter, in the sacraments of the church, and in our denomination at weddings.

PEOPLE: We dedicate these paraments.

MINISTER: The paraments set forth Sunday by Sunday, in a quiet and dignified way, the wonder of God's love and providence. They graphically portray the divine mission in the world of people and bid all to heed the call of God.

PEOPLE: We dedicate these paraments.

DEDICATORY PRAYER: Almighty God, without whom no word or work of ours is possible, but who does accept the gifts of our hands for the beautifying of your sanctuary: bestow your blessing upon us now as we dedicate these memorials and gifts to your glory, for the use of adornment of this holy place. Accept them all, we pray, as we set them apart from common and unhallowed uses, ever to be devoted to the service of your church and the honor of our Lord Jesus Christ, in whose name we ask it. Amen.

As used in the Gunton Temple Memorial Presbyterian Church, Washington, D.C. Eric Lindsay Cowall, minister.

15

Dedication of Altar Memorial Vases

MINISTER: It is our pleasure today to accept and dedicate the altar vases presented with the beautiful floral offering. On behalf of the congregation, I accept this memorial gift with our sincere appreciation and the assurance that not only will it help to perpetuate the memory of those who have given the gift, but also it will add beauty and dignity to our chancel and altar, and add grace to the worship we offer to God and to God's Son, our Lord. I invite you to participate in the consecration of this memorial.

THE SERVICE OF ACCEPTANCE AND DEDICATION

MINISTER: With gratitude to one who through many years has given (herself/himself) with unfailing devotion to this church of which we are a part,

PEOPLE: We accept this gift.

MINISTER: To the glory of God who filled the earth with grace and fragrance, and has brightened the land with the fairness of flowers,

PEOPLE: We dedicate this gift.

MINISTER: With devotion to our Lord Jesus Christ who considered the meaning of the lilies, and found in the humblest flowers the holiest messages,

PEOPLE: We dedicate this gift.

MINISTER: To call attention to the quiet uplift and comfort of the Holy Spirit, seeking to implant more of the beauty of holiness in the hearts of people,

PEOPLE: We dedicate these vases.

MINISTER: To the hope that our prayers may be helped to ascend like garlands of beauty, and our worship be made fragrant with true devotion and consecration,

PEOPLE: We dedicate this gift.

PRAYER OF DEDICATION: Almighty God, who has given and does restore to us those whom we delight to hold in memory, and who having created the great temple of all life, endowing it with the endless beauties of nature, and lacks nothing, yet desires our worship in the sanctuary, accept, we beseech you, the offering of these vases and these flowers, consecrating them by your power and blessing to holy use; and may all who worship here in these days and in the days to come, find inspiration therein, and be lifted up toward you, the source and summit of all being and beauty. We ask in the name of Jesus Christ our Lord. Amen.

As used in the First Congregational Church, Coloma, Michigan. Ralph W. Everroad, minister.

16

Dedication of a Chalice

MINISTER: To Christ, who is our Savior and our Lord,

PEOPLE: We dedicate this cup, which is called a chalice, because it is directed to holy use.

MINISTER: This is the cup of remembrance. When it is used, we will remember the last meal our Lord had with his disciples, in which a cup was passed from one to the other as our Lord said, "Do this in remembrace of me."

PEOPLE: May this cup always help us remember that, O Lord.

MINISTER: This is the cup of agony, and our use of it will cause us to recall our Lord's agony in Gethsemane, when he prayed, " 'My Father, if it be possible, let this cup pass from me' " (Matthew 26:39). And we will remember that sometimes God calls us to agony.

PEOPLE: May this thought ever be in our minds, O Lord.

MINISTER: This is the cup of dedication, and when we use it we will offer ourselves to drink from the cup of faith, allowing our Lord to lead us, and we will not hold back.

PEOPLE: Help us to make this a true promise, O Lord.

MINISTER: This is the cup of forgiveness. Each time that we see it, we ask to be moved to seek your forgiveness, O God.

PEOPLE: And we ask for the ability to forgive others.

MINISTER: This is the cup of fellowship, as people have been brought into loving togetherness when receiving the contents of cups like this;

PEOPLE: And so, O Lord, may we be drawn closer together each time this cup is used.

MINISTER: To these purposes we consecrate this chalice, in memory of your devoted servant. (*Here may be stated the names of those in whose memory this chalice has been given.*)
PEOPLE: Amen.

As used in Salem United Church of Christ, Evansville, Indiana.

17

Dedication of Communion Ware

MINISTER: That the ordinance of the Lord's Supper may be observed with appropriate beauty and dignity,

PEOPLE: We dedicate this Communion ware.

MINISTER: That whenever we see the bread on these plates we may recall our Lord who said, "I am the bread of life,"

PEOPLE: We dedicate these Communion plates.

MINISTER: That as we take bread from these plates we may be reminded of the body of our Lord which was broken for our sake,

PEOPLE: We dedicate these Communion plates.

MINISTER: That whenever we see these Communion trays and receive from them our cup, we may be reminded of the blood of our Lord which was poured out on our behalf,

PEOPLE: We dedicate these Communion trays.

MINISTER: That when we see the cross on the cover of these trays we may recall the sacrifice of our Lord, and consider that from his cross we may draw strength to help us in time of need to bear our own burdens,

PEOPLE: We dedicate these Communion trays.

MINISTER: That the memory of (*here may be stated the name or names of the individuals so memorialized*), whose names appear on the Communion tray covers, may be perpetuated by the use of these beautiful articles,

PEOPLE: We dedicate this Communion ware.

PRAYER (*in unison*): Our God in heaven, we thank you for this simple memorial act by which we remember our Lord Jesus

Christ, and in remembering him also remember the one(s) who served this church so long and faithfully. We thank you for the concern of the deacons and deaconesses who prepare our service with care and dignity. We offer to you our new Communion ware, and with it would dedicate ourselves to a sincere seeking of your Spirit, through the observance of our Lord's Supper, through Jesus Christ our Lord. Amen.

As used in First Baptist Church, Wildwood, New Jersey. J. Francis Peak, minister.

18

Dedication of Cross and Candlesticks

MINISTER: We come to this moment in our worship when we pause to meditate upon the thoughtfulness of others, whose love for their dearly departed ones will be kept fresh by a living memorial to them. Their generosity to us makes possible a more beautiful house of worship. It will make the experience of worship more meaningful to us all, and will serve as a constant reminder that our faith is best carried on when we serve in the spirit of the cross, undergirded by our prayers that rise continually before God as the cloud of smoke that ascends from the candlestick.

We are most grateful for those who have made these living memorials possible. That we may be reminded of him who said, " 'If any one would come after me, let him deny himself and take up his cross and follow me' " (Mark 8:34),

PEOPLE: We dedicate this cross.

MINISTER: That we may exemplify the spirit of the one who spoke, " 'Far be it from me to glory except in the cross of our Lord Jesus Christ' " (Galatians 6:14),

PEOPLE: We dedicate this cross.

MINISTER: And that we may live our Christian faith according to the words of God, "who for the joy that was set before him endured the cross, despising the shame, and is seated at the right hand of the throne of God" (Hebrews 12:2),

PEOPLE: We dedicate this cross.

MINISTER: In the spirit of our Lord who said, ". . . men light a lamp and put it . . . on a stand, and it gives light to all in the house" (Matthew 5:15) and, "let your light so shine before men, that they may see your good works and give glory to your Father who is in heaven" (Matthew 5:16),

PEOPLE: We dedicate this cross.

MINISTER: That we might be reminded that the church must give forth its light, and that judgment comes to the church which does not have its lamps burning by having its candlestick removed,

PEOPLE: We dedicate this cross.

ALL: As the continual burning of the lamp was symbolic of the continuing prosperity of the individual or the family, so may the burning of these candles call us to the continuing prosperity of all that wait before God.

DEDICATORY PRAYER

DEDICATORY HYMN

In the cross of Christ I glory
Tow'ring o'er the wrecks of time;
All the light of sacred story
Gathers round its head sublime.
Bane and blessing, pain and pleasure,
By the cross are sanctified;
Peace is there, that knows no measure,
Joys that through all time abide. Amen.

As used in the Overland Christian Church, Overland, Missouri. Nelson Schuster, minister.

19

Litany for Dedication of Candelabra

MINISTER: The gifts we are about to dedicate to the glory of God and the service of this church have been given by a person who wishes to remain unnamed. The Scripture in Revelation 19:12 speaks for this person when it says, "He has a name written that no one knows but himself." One thing we can say about this person is that, according to John 5:35, "He was a burning and shining lamp, and you were willing to rejoice for a while in his light." Jesus said, " 'Let your light shine,' " and this person will continue to shine in our church as we light the candles Sunday after Sunday to the glory of God. As the acolytes light the candles of our candelabra, let us think about references in the Bible that speak to us about light.

(Acolytes light the first candle in each candelabrum.)

MINISTER: "The true light that enlightens every man was coming into the world" (John 1:9).
PEOPLE: Christ, the Light of the world, is risen and has brought life and immortality to light.

(Acolytes light the second candle in each candelabrum.)

MINISTER: "For once you were darkness, but now you are light in the Lord; walk as children of light" (Ephesians 5:8).
PEOPLE: Christ, the Light of the world, is risen and has brought life and immortality to light.

(Acolytes light the third candle in each candelabrum.)

MINISTER: "Let us then cast off the works of darkness and put on the armour of light" (Romans 13:12).

PEOPLE: Christ, the Light of the world, is risen and has brought life and immortality to light.

(*Acolytes light the fourth candle in each candelabrum.*)

MINISTER: "God, who said, 'Let light shine out of darkness,' who has shone in our hearts to give the light of the knowledge of the glory of God in the face of Christ" (2 Corinthians 4:6).

PEOPLE: Christ, the Light of the world, is risen and has brought life and immortality to light.

(*Acolytes light the fifth candle in each candelabrum.*)

MINISTER: "For once you were darkness, but now you are light in the Lord; walk as children of light; (for the fruit of the light is found in all that is good and right and true)" (Ephesians 5:8-9).

PEOPLE: Christ, the Light of the world, is risen and has brought life and immortality to light.

(*Acolytes light the sixth candle in each candelabrum.*)

MINISTER: "In the midst of a crooked and perverse generation . . . you shine as lights in the world" (Philippians 2:15).

PEOPLE: Christ, the Light of the world, is risen and has brought life and immortality to light.

(*Acolytes light the seventh candle in each candelabrum.*)

MINISTER: "The path of the righteous is like the light of dawn, which shines brighter and brighter until full day" (Proverbs 4:18).

PEOPLE: Christ, the Light of the world, is risen and has brought life and immortality to light.

PRAYER (*in unison*): Eternal God, use the candelabra to illumine our spirits and remind us each Sunday when they are used to "walk in the Light" as followers of Jesus Christ, seeking daily to "let our light shine that people may see our good deeds and glorify our God, in the Spirit of Jesus Christ, our Lord." Amen.

As used at St. Andrew's United Methodist Church, Palo Alto, California. Lester L. Haws, minister.

20

Dedication of Baptismal Font or Baptistry

MINISTER: Praise God in the holy place. Praise be to God, our Creator, Redeemer, Lord, and Sustainer, whom we worship in spirit and truth.

PEOPLE: We come now to dedicate this baptismal font/baptistry to the glory of God.

MINISTER: Christ has commissioned his church to teach all people, baptizing them in the name of the Father, and of the Son, and of the Holy Spirit.

PEOPLE: We dedicate this baptismal font/baptistry to the praise of our Lord, and to the blessing of God's church.

MINISTER: Baptism signifies a believer's union with Christ Jesus through repentance and faith.

PEOPLE: We dedicate this font/baptistry to those whose sins are forgiven, who desire the Holy Spirit's ministry in their lives, and who wish to serve and glorify Christ through Christ's church.

MINISTER: Through baptism we are buried with Christ into his death, and raised to newness of life. The old has passed away, and we now behold that all things have become new.

PEOPLE: We dedicate this font/baptistry to those who seek another beginning, a new lease on life, a fresh page in their personal biography and spiritual pilgrimage.

MINISTER: Baptism marks us as belonging to Christ, his family, his church. The believer is loved by Christ as a son or daughter, and loved by the church family as a brother or sister.

PEOPLE: We dedicate this font/baptistry to those who wish to belong, who wish to be part of a caring family, who wish to be loved and appreciated.

MINISTER: When we are Christ's and he is ours, his Holy Spirit accompanies us in every way of life, giving us companionship, peace, joy, love, and the power to live victoriously, abundantly, and richly.

PEOPLE: We dedicate this font/baptistry to those who prefer not to live alone, but who wish to live life aided, accompanied, supported, loved, and empowered.

MINISTER: We are deeply grateful for those persons who made this font/baptistry possible.

PEOPLE: We dedicate this baptismal font/baptistry to the memory of (*here may be stated the names of those memorialized*), whom we will always love and cherish.

ALL: May our light so shine before all people, that they may see our good works, and glorify our God who is in heaven, to whom be all honor and praise, now and forever more, world without end.

As used in Meadowlark Community Church, San Marcos, California. David Plank, minister.

21

Litany for Dedication of New Offering Plates

MINISTER: O God, the power to obtain wealth, and to share it properly with others, comes to us from you. Money is stored-up spiritual energy which, when used with loving concern, multiplies human joy. Therefore,

PEOPLE: To you, O God, owner of all our possessions, we dedicate these offering plates.

MINISTER: Because money helps to provide for a pastor's services and for the supplying of a congregation's material and spiritual needs,

PEOPLE: To you, O God, owner of all our possessions, we dedicate these offering plates.

MINISTER: Because the gifts placed herein by thoughtful members will relieve the plight of the needy,

PEOPLE: To you, O God, owner of all our possessions, we dedicate these offering plates.

MINISTER: Because by giving we help unfortunate and under-privileged persons of every race and color in our country and throughout the world,

PEOPLE: To you, O God, owner of all our possessions, we dedicate these offering plates.

MINISTER: Because the presentation of this lovely gift brings tender memories of a (brother/sister) greatly beloved,

ALL: To you, O God, creator of our lives and owner of all our possessions, we dedicate these offering plates to the memory of (*here may be stated the name of the person memorialized*) with gratitude and appreciation.

As used in the Williamsbridge Road Reformed Church, Bronx, New York. Millard M. Gifford, minister.

22

Litany for the Dedication of Candlelighters

MINISTER: Candlelighters have been presented to this congregation by (*here may be stated the name of the donors*) in memory of (*here may be stated the names of those to be memorialized*). Moses was instructed by God to " 'make a lampstand of hammered work . . . and there shall be six branches going out of its sides' " (Exodus 25:31-33). He was also told to " 'put the lampstand in the tent of meeting opposite the table' " (Exodus 40:24). Having the candelabra properly situated with candles ready to be lighted to bring symbolically the Light of the Word, Jesus Christ, to illuminate our service of worship, we now present to this congregation these candlelighters in memory of (*here may be stated the names of those to be memorialized by this gift*).

LIGHTING OF THE CANDLES

(*Candles are lighted on each candelabra as selected readers read the following.*)

FIRST READER: We light the first candle with the thought of the ancient psalmist: "Yea, thou dost light my lamp; the LORD my God lightens my darkness" (Psalm 18:28).

SECOND READER: We touch the flame to the second candle as we hear Job say: " 'Oh, that I were as in the months of old, as in the days when God watched over me; when his lamp shone upon my head, and by his light I walked through darkness' " (Job 29:2-3).

THIRD READER: As we light the third candle, we remember

that the psalmist said: "Yea, thou dost light my lamp, the LORD my God lightens my darkness" (Psalm 18:28).

FOURTH READER: As we light the fourth candle, we hear Jesus, in the Sermon on the Mount, say, " 'Nor do men light a lamp and put it under a bushel, but on a stand, and it gives light to all in the house' " (Matthew 5:15).

FIFTH READER: As we light the fifth candle, remember that Jesus also said, " 'If then your whole body is full of light, having no part dark, it will be wholly bright, as when a lamp with its rays gives you light' " (Luke 11:3).

SIXTH READER: In lighting the sixth candle, we are reminded that Paul wrote to the Corinthians: "For it is the God who said, 'Let light shine out of darkness,' who has shone in our hearts to give the light of the knowledge of the glory of God in the face of Christ" (2 Corinthians 4:6).

SEVENTH READER: As we light the seventh candle, we think of the words of Paul to the Ephesians: "For once you were in darkness, but now you are light in the Lord; walk as children of light, for the fruit of light is found in all that is good and right and true" (Ephesians 5:8-9).

PRAYER OF DEDICATION: Eternal God, we thank you for the lives of (*here may be stated the names of those memorialized*). We thank you that they did let their light of faith in Jesus Christ shine before people that they might see their good deeds and glorify their God in heaven. As we light the candles on our altar from Sunday to Sunday, may we light our candles of faith in Jesus Christ, as they did, that we may reflect your light of goodness, righteousness, and truth, in our lives. Continue to send forth your light and your truth through us, forever and ever. Amen.

As used at Point Pleasant United Methodist Church, Elk Grove, California. Lester L. Haws, minister.

23

Dedication of a Pulpit Bible

MINISTER: In honor of God, the Almighty, who created us and gave us the priceless gift of speech,

PEOPLE: We dedicate this pulpit Bible.

MINISTER: In praise of Jesus Christ, the Incarnate Word, who spoke with matchless power and grace,

PEOPLE: We dedicate this pulpit Bible.

MINISTER: In remembrance of the Holy Spirit, who speaks to the hidden things in our hearts,

PEOPLE: We dedicate this pulpit Bible.

MINISTER: For all those who were inspired to write and to translate the sacred Scriptures,

PEOPLE: We dedicate this pulpit Bible.

MINISTER: In order that our children may know of the life of Christ and understand his message,

PEOPLE: We dedicate this pulpit Bible.

MINISTER: So that our young people may receive direction, comfort, and counsel from the best religious wisdom of our faith,

PEOPLE: We dedicate this pulpit Bible.

MINISTER: So that we all may have the comforting assurance of pardon and forgiveness, and be encouraged to walk in newness of life,

PEOPLE: We dedicate this pulpit Bible.

MINISTER: To the glory of God, the enlightenment of this congregation, the strengthening of the ties which bind us to all people, this pulpit Bible is now dedicated. May humble tongues proclaim its imperishable truths and receptive hearts receive the message it imparts.

ALL: Almighty God who has spoken to us through the Holy Word, we thank you for this gift and beseech you to bless and sanctify it. May those who read from it in the appointed services of our church and the congregations who hear it, receive the fullest blessing of your love. May its eternal message serve as a lamp unto our feet as we travel through darkened places. May its inspiration lift us when we feel discouraged and downtrodden. May it reflect our lives in the light of the life of our Lord Jesus Christ in whose name we pray. Amen.

As used in First Church Congregational, Painesville, Ohio. William T. Griffiths, minister.

24

Organ Dedication and Celebration

PRELUDE

RESPONSIVE CALL TO WORSHIP

MINISTER: "O sing to the LORD a new song, for he has done marvelous things!" (Psalm 98:1).

PEOPLE: Sing for joy to the Lord, all the earth!

MINISTER: Praise him with songs and shouts of joy!

PEOPLE: Sing praises to the Lord! Play music on the organ!

MINISTER: Blow trumpets and horns,

PEOPLE: And shout for joy to the Lord!

HYMN: "Praise to the Lord, the Almighty"

PRAYER OF THANKSGIVING: Our Lord and God, we thank you for this day which you have made. We thank you for all the people whom you have loved and given us to love. We thank you for the gifts of song and organ with which we may voice our praise. Bless us, O God, and help us learn to be grateful, responsible, and loving. May we become more fully aware of and responsive to your greatest gift of all, your love made visible to us through Jesus Christ.

SILENT PRAYER

THE LORD'S PRAYER

ANTHEM

PRESENTATION OF THE ORGAN: We present this organ to be dedicated to the glory of God, to the upbuilding of human life, and to the service of the church.

ACT OF DEDICATION

MINISTER: To the glory of God who calls us by grace; to the honor of the Son, who loves us and gave himself for us; to the praise of the Holy Spirit who lives in us and recreates us, we dedicate this organ.

PEOPLE: "Praise God in his sanctuary. Praise him in his mighty firmament . . . Praise him with the trumpet sound; praise him with lute and harp" (Psalm 150:1,3).

MINISTER: We dedicate this organ to God for the proclamation of the gospel, the Good News; for the worship of God through music; for the nurture and instruction of children, youth, and adults in God's way of truth and love; for the expression of the beauty of holiness; for the celebration of God's presence in the sanctuary and in all of life.

PEOPLE: Praise God with stringed instruments and organ! Let everything that has breath praise the Lord!

MINISTER: We dedicate this organ to the healing of life's discords, and the revelation of the hidden soul of harmony; to the lifting of the depressed and the comforting of the sorrowing; to the humbling of the heart before eternal mysteries, and the lifting of the soul to abiding beauty and joy, by the gospel of infinite love and good will.

PEOPLE: "That at the name of Jesus every knee should bow, in heaven and on earth and under the earth, and every tongue confess that Jesus Christ is Lord, to the glory of God the Father" (Philippians 2:10-11).

MINISTER: In thankfulness for the love so graciously expressed in sacrificial giving; in loving remembrance of those who have been memorialized; in gratitude for the labors of all who love and serve Christ through his church here and everywhere, we dedicate this organ.

PEOPLE: We, the people of this congregation, surrounded by a great cloud of witnesses, thankful for our heritage and sensitive to the sacrifices of those who have gone this way before us, dedicate ourselves anew to the worship and service of God, through Jesus Christ our Lord. Amen.

HYMN: "When Morning Gilds the Skies"
OFFERING
ANTHEM
SCRIPTURE: 1 Corinthians 3:16-4:11
SERMON

HYMN: "O for a Thousand Tongues to Sing"
BENEDICTION AND RESPONSE: "God Be with You"
POSTLUDE

As used in Brooklyn United Methodist Church, Brooklyn, Pennsylvania.

25

Dedication of a Piano

MINISTER: We rejoice today in the dedication of this instrument of music to the ministry of melody and harmony among all who assemble here.

PEOPLE: For the joy and the enrichment of the souls of the men and women of this (village/church), we dedicate this instrument.

MINISTER: From the earliest periods of the world's history, music has been a medium of worship; from the days of the crudest harps to our own time, deep emotions have been stirred by vibrating strings.

PEOPLE: We dedicate this instrument as a medium of inspiration and beauty.

MINISTER: The souls of master musicians have been poured out through stirring concertos, great hymns, and moving symphonies; thereby the lives of men and women have been lifted with the sweet sounds of music.

PEOPLE: Therefore, O God, we dedicate this instrument to the appreciation of the highest and best in music among your people here.

MINISTER: That the message and meaning of music in this congregation may be to the glory of God, let us dedicate this piano.

PEOPLE: To the glory of God, the Almighty One, that we may more readily worship God, we dedicate this piano.

MINISTER: To the praise of the great Galilean at whose birth the angels sang, that our joy in him may find more meaning, we dedicate this piano.

PEOPLE: And to the Holy Spirit, in whose fellowship the discords of life are lost in the glorious harmony of God's love, we dedicate this piano.

MINISTER: That blessing and joy may come to all who have eagerly shared in this day's dream, having gladly presented their gifts to make it a reality.   u.T.M.C.

PEOPLE: That those who come to this (village/church) may be comforted in sorrow, strengthened in weakness, and encouraged in despair, we dedicate this piano.

Unison PRAYER OF DEDICATION: We praise and thank you, God, for the gift of music. Through us, as channels of your grace, may this blessed legacy be shared with all mankind. Grant that we may exemplify in our own lives the harmony of your great purpose for us. Give us magnitude of soul and understanding hearts, that we who make music may be players upon rightly tuned instruments responding to your leading. Let us with renewed consecration dedicate ourselves to the purpose of bringing the spiritualizing force of music to the inner life of ourselves and neighbors here in our church and community.

As used in Bristol Village, Waverly, Ohio. Written by John Glenn.

26

Dedication of a Church Bell

ACCEPTANCE OF THE BELL

MINISTER: On behalf of this congregation I accept this gift of this lovely bell. It will be a fitting and loving memorial to our beloved (sister/brother), who was a faithful member of this congregation. The bell will add beauty, meaning, and inspiration to our worship; it will announce to this community Sunday by Sunday that we are gathered here to God's glory; and by its ringing it will invite whosoever will to join us in our fellowship of love and service.

THE ACT OF DEDICATION

MINISTER: In deepest appreciation for the life and love of the one who is memorialized by every use of this bell,

PEOPLE: We accept this gift as an instrument of remembrance.

MINISTER: With sincere gratitude to all whose generosity and loving remembrance have made this gift possible,

PEOPLE: We accept this bell as an instrument of thanksgiving.

MINISTER: To announce to every person in tones clear and sure the Good News of God's love shown us in Jesus, and the invitation to follow him,

PEOPLE: We now dedicate this bell as an instrument of witness.

MINISTER: To kindle a spirit of reverence and devotion in the hearts of us gathered here for worship, and to summon us to enter his presence with joyful and expectant hearts,

PEOPLE: We dedicate this bell as an instrument of praise.

MINISTER: To remind all who hear its sound that here there is comfort for the sorrowing, strength for the weak, cheer for the downcast, hope for the despairing, and friendship for the forlorn,

PEOPLE: We dedicate this bell as an instrument of love.

As used at Meadowlark Community Church, San Marcos, California. David Plank, minister.

27

Dedication of a Carillon

MINISTER: Forasmuch as by the generosity of (*name of donor*) these new bells have been provided as an aid to our worship of God, and as an invitation to all who hear to come and worship, it is right that we should now dedicate to God these bells and set them apart to the holy use for which they are designed. To the glory of God, author of all beauty and goodness, giver of all skill of mind and hand,

PEOPLE: We dedicate these bells.

MINISTER: In faith in our Lord Jesus Christ, who has inspired us to offer in his presence our best in music,

PEOPLE: We dedicate these bells.

MINISTER: Moved by the Holy Spirit, our guide in the worship of God, our inspiration in praise, our helper in the understanding of truth and beauty, love and service,

PEOPLE: We dedicate these bells.

MINISTER: To kindle the flame of devotion and to call by their ringing voices all who hear, to worship Almighty God in spirit and in truth,

PEOPLE: We dedicate these bells.

MINISTER: To ring in joyous affirmation when before the altar of this church a man and woman stand to pledge to each other their deathless affection and thereby to establish a new home where God may be glorified and his name held in honor,

PEOPLE: We dedicate these bells.

MINISTER: To comfort the sorrowful, to cheer the faint, to

bring peace and love to human hearts, and to lead all who hear into the way of eternal life,

PEOPLE: We dedicate these bells.

MINISTER: To the glory of God and in loving memory,

PEOPLE: We dedicate these bells.

ALL: O God, most holy and most high, unto whom we have access by one spirit through our Lord Jesus Christ; we give unto you praise and honor and worship. We thank you that you have made us so that music can lift our hearts and minds to you. Grant that we and all who hereafter shall hear the music of these bells shall be moved to love you more, serve you better, worship you, praise you, and pray to you more regularly, led and inspired by the Holy Spirit. This we ask in the name of our Lord Jesus Christ. Amen. Blessing and glory, wisdom and thanksgiving, honor and power and might be unto our God for ever and ever. Amen.

As used in the University Christian Church, Fort Worth, Texas. Granville T. Walker, minister.

28

Dedication Service for Handbells

MINISTER: Acting for this congregation, I accept the gift of these beautiful handbells with appreciation to all who contributed toward their purchase and with the assurance that not only will they help to memorialize our longtime friend and faithful member (*name of person to be memorialized*), but also that these bells will speak with clarity and purity—qualities not unlike those in the life of the one they memorialize—adding beauty and grace to the worship of God, and giving an opportunity for many to grow in their ability to serve God and worthily to magnify God's name. I invite all present to participate in the consecration of this memorial.

THE SOUND OF THE HANDBELLS (*Handbell Choir performs*)

THE ACT OF DEDICATION

MINISTER: With gratitude to those who have made this gift, and in appreciation for the life which is memorialized by it by each use of these handbells,

PEOPLE: We accept this gift.

MINISTER: To the glory of God who inspired men and women to use their abilities to bring order to bear upon sound to create music,

PEOPLE: We dedicate these handbells.

MINISTER: With devotion to our Lord Jesus Christ who has led us to know God and brought us to know that in unity and in harmony we may perform a higher service and more perfectly fulfill the will of God,

PEOPLE: We dedicate these handbells.

MINISTER: To enable our children, youth, and adults to find a purposeful way of service and a more meaningful expression of their devotion,

PEOPLE: We dedicate these handbells.

MINISTER: To sound to every person in clear and ringing tones the eternal message of God's love and the invitation of Christ to follow his way to God,

PEOPLE: We dedicate these handbells.

PRAYER OF DEDICATION: Almighty God, who has given and who restores to us those we delight to hold in memory, we recognize that you are the creator of all things and in need of nothing, yet we desire to worship you in the sanctuary. Accept, we pray, the offering of these handbells, and the lives which have been given to you in them, and consecrate them by your power and blessing to holy use. May all who worship here now and in the years to come, find inspiration by their use and be lifted up toward you, the source of all being and beauty. This prayer we offer in the name of Jesus Christ our Lord. Amen.

As used in Watson Terrace Christian Church, St. Louis, Missouri. John L. Bray, minister.

29

Dedication of Hymnals

CALL TO WORSHIP
MINISTER: "It is good to give thanks to the LORD,
PEOPLE: "To sing praises to your name, O Most High.
MINISTER: "To declare your steadfast love in the morning,
PEOPLE: "And your faithfulness by night,
MINISTER: "To the music of the lute and the harp,
PEOPLE: "To the melody of the lyre.
MINISTER: "For you, O LORD, have made me glad by your
   work;
PEOPLE: "At the works of your hands I sing for joy" (Psalm
   92:1-4).
PROCESSIONAL HYMN: "O for a Thousand Tongues to Sing"

A LITANY OF PRAISE (*to retire the old hymnals*)

MINISTER: The day of dedication has long passed; the hours
   of service have been many and praiseworthy; their spiritual
   messages uplifting.
PEOPLE: God's name has been praised.
MINISTER: Because the poetic words have flowed smoothly
   and effectively into our hearts from the heart of God's ded-
   icated poets,
PEOPLE: God's name has been praised.
MINISTER: Because inspired congregations have rejoiced in
   song, life has been lived on a higher plane,
PEOPLE: We offer unto God our gratitude.
MINISTER: Remembering those in whose names these books

of worship have been memorialized and wishing to continue this memorial, we will present them to their remaining families.

PEOPLE: Thanks be to God for those so memorialized.

HYMN: "Blest Be the Tie That Binds"

(The old hymnals are collected from the people.)

ORGAN VOLUNTARY

PRAYER OF GRATEFUL MEMORIES

(The ushers present the old hymnals at the altar.)

MINISTER: We are grateful, O God, for the inspiring words and music that have brought us hours of joy, comfort and courage.

DEDICATION OF NEW HYMNALS

LITANY OF DEDICATION

MINISTER: Almighty God, who has set forth the Good News in Jesus Christ and put into our hearts a new song,

PEOPLE: We offer to you our sacrifice of praise.

MINISTER: For your children who through the universal language of poetry and melody have taught us to sing your praise,

PEOPLE: We offer you our gratitude.

MINISTER: For our forebears in the faith who set the world to singing and who gave the people of our church a sacred heritage of song,

PEOPLE: We praise your holy name.

MINISTER: For the joy you have kindled in the hearts of your children, expressing itself in song and calling us to faith in your Son,

PEOPLE: We bless your name, O Lord.

MINISTER: For this new hymnal and all whose dedicated efforts have made it possible,

PEOPLE: We give you thanks, O Lord.

MINISTER: O God, whose purpose is the redemption of your world, use this gift to high and holy purposes that it may enable those who seek to worship you in spirit and in truth to express gratitude, penitence, and commitment,

PEOPLE: We humbly beseech you, O Lord.

MINISTER: May it cause a new song to rise from the hearts of those who dwell in cities, in the farmland, and the mountains, from near and far around the earth,

PEOPLE: We humbly beseech you, O Lord.

MINISTER: May this hymnal provide marching music for your church,

PEOPLE: And may our lives be dedicated so that your kingdom may come and your will be done on earth as it is in heaven.

PRAYER OF DEDICATION: Grant, O Lord, that the harmony from these songs of praise may enter our lives and help us more fully be dedicated to your name. May we be more sensitive to the warmth they hold, the courage they possess, and the truth they tell. Amen.

ORGAN VOLUNTARY (*The ushers distribute the new hymnals to the congregation.*)

HYMN: "Come, We That Love the Lord"

SCRIPTURE READING

SERMON

OFFERING AND OFFERTORY

BENEDICTION AND DOXOLOGY

As used at Lakewood United Methodist Church, Lakewood, Ohio. Leonard H. Budd, minister.

30

Dedication of Choir Robes

MINISTER: "O come, let us sing unto the LORD, let us make a joyful noise to the rock of our salvation!

PEOPLE: "Let us come into his presence with thanksgiving; let us make a joyful noise to him with songs of praise!" (Psalm 95:1-2).

MINISTER: "O sing to the LORD a new song, for [the Lord] has done marvelous things! His right hand and his holy arm have gotten him victory" (Psalm 98:1).

PEOPLE: "Make a joyful noise to the LORD, all the earth; break forth into joyous song and sing praises!

MINISTER: "Sing praises to the LORD with the lyre, with the lyre and the sound of melody!" (Psalm 98:4-5).

PEOPLE: "I will sing to the LORD as long as I live; I will sing praise to my God while I have being" (Psalm 104:33).

MINISTER: "Sing to him, sing praises to him, tell of all his wonderful works!" (Psalm 105:2).

PEOPLE: "I will sing a new song to thee, O God; upon a ten-stringed harp I will play to thee" (Psalm 144:9).

MINISTER: Let everything that has breath praise the Lord.

PEOPLE: We praise you, O God, in your sanctuary, we praise you in the firmament of your power. We praise you, O Lord.

LITANY OF DEDICATION

MINISTER: To the glory of God and to the singing of praises to God's holy name,

PEOPLE: We dedicate these robes.

MINISTER: To the enrichment of our corporate worship experience,

PEOPLE: We dedicate these robes.

MINISTER: To the end that we may forget human personality and see only God in the music of our worship service,

PEOPLE: We dedicate these robes.

MINISTER: To the end that unity and harmony of human voices, blended together into a choir, might portray to us the personal unity and harmony that is possible with God,

PEOPLE: We dedicate these robes.

MINISTER: To the holy purposes of God revealed to us in the worship experience of the church, drawing us into a more intimate, personal relationship with God, Christ, and the Holy Spirit,

PEOPLE: We dedicate these robes.

PRAYER OF DEDICATION (*in unison*): O Lord our God, whose name is excellent and whose glory is above the earth and heaven, we beseech you to bless these your servants who sing praises to your holy name, and these robes that they are wearing. To them has been given the sacred trust of leading the praises of your people in the sanctuary. As you have called them to this service, make and keep them worthy of this calling. Let the Holy Spirit rule in their hearts as they carry out this sacred trust. May they lead others to offer their worship in reverence, and to sing with the understanding and the heart, as unto you and not unto people. Grant that they may be as one with your people in their love for your house and their fellowship in your service, that all of us may find joy and increase of faith in praising your wonderful and holy name.

Bless these robes and the holy purposes to which they are dedicated this day. Bless those in whose precious memory they are given to this church. Bless those who wear these robes through the years, that they may never lose sight of this gracious privilege coming to them from our God. In your great mercy grant that all who learn here to find joy in worshiping you, may be numbered at last with those who shall sing a new song before your heavenly throne, through Jesus Christ our Lord, who is worshiped and glorified with you, O God, and the Holy Spirit, world without end. Amen.

As used in West Creighton Avenue Christian Church, Fort Wayne, Indiana. Donald H. McCord, minister. Elyse K. Williamson, associate.

31

Dedication of Chair Lift/Elevator

MINISTER: Every good gift and every perfect gift is from above, coming down from God.

PEOPLE: "Lift up your heads, O gates! and be lifted up, O ancient doors! that the King of glory may come in.

MINISTER: "Who is the King of glory?

PEOPLE: "The LORD, strong and mighty, the LORD, mighty in battle!" (Psalm 24:7-8).

ALL: O, come to our church, Lord Jesus, there is room in our edifice for you.

MINISTER: Let us have thankfulness that our vision is so inclusive that we want to make our structure pleasing to God and available to all God's children.

PEOPLE: God is no respecter of persons. All are God's children and God's love encircles each one. God would have each and all know the love, the greatness, the goodness of God.

DEDICATION OF CHAIR LIFT/ELEVATOR

MINISTER: For the faith of the pioneers in our community who built this sanctuary at this spot, and for fidelity to those who through the decades have been solicitous that all may have access to its facilities,

PEOPLE: We thank you, Lord.

MINISTER: For the vision of those who felt the need for this chair lift/elevator and have worked to make it possible that those who have need for its use can come into the sanctuary and find inspiration and stimulus,

PEOPLE: We thank you, O God. We dedicate to you, O God, this evidence of goodwill and guidance for all who may utilize this facility. May it bring blessing to any who are handicapped that they may enter into and worship in this house of God. May your name be exalted through the efforts of all who pass this way.

DEDICATORY PRAYER
HYMN: "Blest Be the Tie That Binds"
BENEDICTION

(A demonstration of the chair lift/elevator may then be given by a handicapped person as the people exit from the sanctuary.)

As used at Albright United Methodist Church, Milwaukee, Wisconsin.

32

Dedication of Christian and National Flags

ALL: In the name of God the Almighty, and of the Son, and of the Holy Spirit. Amen.

MINISTER: To the glory of God and our spiritual enrichment,

PEOPLE: To you, we dedicate these flags.

MINISTER: That all who worship here may be reminded of the religious freedom and tolerance for which it stands,

PEOPLE: To you, we dedicate this American flag.

MINISTER: As a visible emblem that we serve him who said, "Follow me,"

PEOPLE: To you, we dedicate this Christian flag.

MINISTER: That it may always bring to our minds the watchful providence of the God who guards the country for which it stands,

PEOPLE: To you, we dedicate this American flag.

MINISTER: That its presence here may help to keep us close to God in whom alone we have hope of life and happiness,

PEOPLE: To you, we dedicate this Christian flag.

MINISTER: That constantly we may thank God for the sacrificial service of those who endured hardship and suffering to bring it into being,

PEOPLE: To you, we dedicate this American flag.

MINISTER: That silently side by side during each service, they may remind us of our duty to God and country, of the love of our Savior and of the freedom of our nation,

PEOPLE: To you, we dedicate these flags.

DEDICATORY PRAYER

SALUTE TO THE CHRISTIAN FLAG

ALL: I pledge allegiance to my flag and to the Savior for whose kingdom it stands; one fellowship uniting all humankind in service and love.

HYMN

Our fathers' God, to Thee,
Author of liberty,
To Thee we sing:
Long may our land be bright
With freedom's holy light;
Protect us by Thy might;
Great God, our King!

SALUTE TO THE AMERICAN FLAG

ALL: I pledge allegiance to the Flag of the United States of America, and to the Republic for which it stands: one Nation under God, indivisible, with liberty and justice for all.

HYMN

My native country, thee,
Land of the noble free,
Thy name I love;
I love thy rocks and rills,
Thy woods and templed hills;
My heart with rapture thrills
Like that above.

33

Litany for a
Manse Site Dedication

MINISTER: In the name of God the Almighty, and of the Son, and of the Holy Spirit. Amen.

PEOPLE: Our help is in the name of the Lord, who made the heavens and the earth.

MINISTER: For the marvelous work of your hands in the creation of all things in heaven and on the earth and under the earth,

PEOPLE: We give you praise, our God and our Creator.

MINISTER: For the excellent grace by which you have supplied all our needs, and have blessed our lives individually and corporately,

PEOPLE: We give you thanks our Maker and Defender.

MINISTER: For the wisdom, generosity, and foresight of the men and women of generations past who founded this congregation and provided for its continuance; for those servants of yours, past and present, who have had a part in bringing us to this moment,

PEOPLE: We give you thanks, O Lord.

MINISTER: In these thoughts of gratitude for your unsearchable goodness to us, we renew ourselves in dedication to your holy purposes, and all that is ours we do so dedicate. To the purpose for which it is now consecrated,

PEOPLE: We dedicate this ground to you, O God.

MINISTER: For the good of our congregation, for the enrichment of its ministry, for the strengthening of your holy church, and to the praise of your name,

PEOPLE: We dedicate this ground, O Lord.
MINISTER: In the name of the almighty One, and of the Son, and of the Holy Spirit.
ALL: Amen.

As used at the United Presbyterian Church, Americus, Kansas. Written by John C. Bush.

34

Dedication of a Parsonage

MINISTER: In the name of God, the Creator, and of the Son, and of the Holy Spirit. Amen.

PEOPLE: We have assembled here to dedicate this house unto God.

TRUSTEES: As those to whom the responsibility of maintaining this house has been committed, we now express our willingness to dedicate it unto him who is the Master Builder, and the keeper of all, whose we are and whom we serve.

MINISTER: To what ends and for what purposes do you wish to dedicate this house?

ALL: As a fitting and pleasant place where our pastor and family can make their home.

As a place where study and meditation on the holy Scriptures may be pursued.

As a place where Christian fellowship may be had, where we may share both our joys and our sorrows, our successes and our shortcomings, and strengthen the ties that bind our hearts in Christian love.

As a place where the confidential counsel of God's ministering servant can be found.

And as a quiet and comfortable place of refuge and relief to which God's servant can return when at times the duties and responsiblities of the office bear heavily.

To these ends and for the glory of God, we now dedicate this parsonage.

MINISTER: O God, you have heard the expressed desires of

these your people for whose spiritual well-being I am responsible. Accept, we ask you, this house which they with their gifts and their labor do provide and shall endeavor to maintain.

Grant indeed, gracious God, that we may all do our part to keep it always for the high purposes to which they have now pledged it. And may all who shall ever dwell herein live lives that bear steadfast witness to the Savior, that your blessed and holy benediction may rest upon it now and as long as it shall stand.

In the name of Jesus Christ, our Lord. Amen.

ALL: Bless this house, O Lord, we pray,
Make it safe by night and day;
Bless these walls, so firm and stout,
Keeping want and trouble out;
Bless the roof and chimney tall,
Let your peace lie over all;
Bless this door, that it may prove
Ever open to joy and love.
Bless the folk who dwell within,
Keep them pure and free from sin;
Bless us all, that we may be
Fit, O Lord, to dwell with thee,
Bless us all that one day we
May dwell, O Lord, with thee. Amen.

(From the song *Bless This House*, music by May H. Brahe, words by Helen Taylor, copyright 1927, 1932, by Boosey and Co., Ltd.; renewed 1954, 1959. Reprinted by permission of Boosey and Hawkes, Inc.)

As used in the Fontana Evangelical United Brethren Church, Lebanon, Pennsylvania. Robert P. Longenecker, minister.

35

Dedication of a Home

MINISTER: Peace be to this house,
PEOPLE: And to all who dwell therein.
MINISTER: Our help is in the name of the Lord,
PEOPLE: Who made heaven and earth.
MINISTER: Peace be within your walls,
PEOPLE: And prosperity within your palaces.
MINISTER: For my brothers', sisters', and friends' sakes, I will now say:
PEOPLE: Peace be with you. Glory be to the Father, and to the Son, and to the Holy Ghost. As it was in the beginning, is now, and ever shall be, world without end. Amen.
SCRIPTURE: Proverbs 24:3-4
MINISTER: Let us pray. O Lord God, your gifts are many and in wisdom you have made all things to give you glory. We ask you to bless those who live in this place. Visit with your love and gladness all who come and go, and preserve us all in peace, through Jesus Christ our Lord. Amen.
A CANDLE IS LIGHTED
SCRIPTURE: Matthew 5:14-16
MINISTER: Let us pray. O God, as this candle gives light to this home, so enable those who dwell here to be your light in the world, through Jesus Christ our Lord. Amen.
SCRIPTURE: Matthew 7:24-27
MINISTER: Let us pray. O God, from whom the whole family in heaven and earth is named, be present in this home, that all who live here, having genuine affection for one other,

may find here a haven of blessing and of peace, through Jesus Christ our Lord. Amen.

SCRIPTURE: Luke 19:1-10

MINISTER: Let us pray. O God, refresh all who visit here, that they may know friendship and love, through Jesus Christ our Lord. Amen.

SCRIPTURE: Psalm 121:8

MINISTER: Let us pray. O God, protect and guide those who live here, their going out and their coming in; and let them share the hospitality of this home with all who visit, that those who enter here may know your love and peace, through Jesus Christ our Lord. Amen.

SCRIPTURE: John 13:34-35

MINISTER: Let us pray. O God, be present with those who come here for fellowship and recreation, that they may be renewed and refreshed, through Jesus Christ our Lord. Amen.

SCRIPTURE: Isaiah 32:17-18

MINISTER: Let us pray. To live with you, O Lord, is to be at home with ourselves. Now be with us, we pray, as we dedicate this place as a home for (*first names of residents may be stated*). Bless these personal things of taste and choice that put the mark of these particular people upon it and make it theirs. May it be a place of shelter and protection, of rest and healing, of warmth and hospitality. And may your embracing love be seen and felt in all the celebrations, daily chores, hard decisions, and shared glories that will occur here. As it will become the storehouse of blessed memories, make it also a place for growth in grace. We pray in the name of him who has prepared a place for us, in whose house are many rooms, even Jesus Christ our Lord. Amen.

LORD'S PRAYER

MINISTER: The Lord watch over our going out and our coming in from this time forth forever. Amen.

DOXOLOGY

(Adapted from *Occasional Services*, copyright 1982, Lutheran Church in America, "Blessing of a Dwelling" and *The Occasional Services*, copyright 1962, The United Lutheran Church in America, "Order for the Blessing of a Dwelling." Used with permission.)

As used in the home of Lois and Manfred Holck, Jr., in Austin, Texas.

Additional Litanies and Services

Ground-Breaking Service in Verse
Prayers for Use in Laying a Cornerstone
Litany for the Dedication of New Church Doors
Dedication of a Steeple and Bell
Cross-Lifting Ceremony
Dedication of Memorial Plantings (Garden)
Dedication of a Clock
Dedication of Appointments and Memorials
Office for the Blessing of an Altar
Dedication of a New Bible Stand
Consecration of Memorial Paraments
Rededication of an Organ
Litany for Dedication of a Sound System
Dedication of Flag and Flagpole
Litany for the Dedication of a Stage
Dedication of Pulpit Chairs
Dedication of a Sanctuary Piano
Litany for the Dedication of Organ Chimes
Dedication of Funeral Pall
Dedication of Acolyte Robes and Stoles
Litany for the Dedication of a Literature Rack
Dedication of a Water Treatment Plant
Litany for the Dedication of a Community Swimming Pool
Services of Dedication of a Community Building and Flagstaff
Service for the Launching of a Ship

Litany for the Dedication of a Hospital
Dedication of a Headstone
Dedication of Church Lawn Plantings
Dedication of Welcome Card Pew Racks
Dedication of Church Office Machines
Dedication of a Movie Projector
A Service for the Burial of Ashes at Sea
Dedication of Church World Service Clothing

A photocopy of any of these services is available from Church Management, Inc., for $2.00 each, postpaid. Send your name and address along with your payment to Church Management, Inc., P. O. Box 1625, Austin, TX 78767.